# MUFFLED VOICES

## CHAMP

# Muffled Voices

By

Champion Muthle

# DEDICATION

For Aung San Suu Kyi.
May your voice be forever unmuffled and free.

# ACKNOWLEDGMENTS

A special thanks to my rescuers and protectors.
To all the countries where voices are free instead of stifled.

Congress and the Constitution are under attack all around the world. Muzzled and muffled are the voices of virtue and reason under a medical face mask. All that remains is confusion, chaos and COVID.

# Muffled Voices

Covid-19 has been a Rorschach Test for the world, and the results are alarming.

There are certain histories that will never be written, and certain histories that couldn't be written fast enough.

I can still hear their sirens ringing in my ears, and I am no safer for it. Traumatized, terrorized, victimized, yes. But safer, absolutely not.

Once you become a Civil Rights Leader the games begin, and we are rarely better off for the playing, if you know what I mean. Thus begins the great sacrifice.

Strategy is the basis of the creative idea; it is the very location of intellectual property. Creative is the icing on the cake...the frosting, if you will.

If politicians paid as much attention to governing as they did to winning elections, the world would be a significantly better place. Once they're in office, it seems, all that goes out the window.

Most music is uninspired sound.
Most writing is just a bunch of words.
Most films are just a selection of images.
Most interaction is just conversation.
We are for Art, Magic, and Inspiration.

Officer. Enlisted Man. Medic.
Lieutenant. Corporal. Captain.
…We are all Generals today.

Our enemy has issued their intentions.
Let us go fast now, to the battlefield.
And issue our reply.

When I told them that they stole my memory, added it to existing knowledge, deleted my identity, and then blamed me for it, they asked: What's your name again?

Life on a string, love on a wire.
Fame, control, and fortune is their desire.

It is not the natural way of space that the world should be forever sinking into darkness. Light alone cannot keep us afloat. Surely we must find some buoy in our own behavior also.

The InterContinental, OR Tambo Airport.
The Double Tree, Minneapolis Minnesota.
Hostel International, San Francisco.
Attacked, ousted, abused.
Roll the footage, please.

14

When the State awakens to its crimes, the whole world shines, and the Devil sleeps.

The budding Journalist is
a blossoming flower.

If you ran the FBIs Security Index backwards many lives might be saved.

It is the great goal of the oppressor to
forever delay and confuse our endeavors.

The Hat in the Cat.
The Pack in the Rat.
It seems our words have become muddled.
It seems our dreams have been befuddled.

Live your life not in spite or jealousy, lest you become the victim of an arbitrary emotion too.

It is a strange reality we find ourselves in today; one not fully governed by Natural Law. This is no doubt the result of our Medical, Legal and Political afflictions. We have abused the Laws of Nature and it is fighting back.

Gossip will have you easily convinced of the opposite. It is perhaps more powerful than propaganda. Always do your own research.

Reward yourself every now and then.
You deserve it.

Society must chisel its way out of its own archeology and be born anew, lest it be forever buried in the sands of its own detritus.

24

Never forget that essence precedes existence, and time is of the essence.

25

Be wary of those fools who wish to disprove their own humanity.

The whole world lives in the wobble, that dance in which the bees delight.

Eyes closed, nothing exists.
Eyes open, life unfolds.

My passport has been stolen
along with my identity.
My birth certificate denied
along with my name.
My Social Security says deceased.
My citizenship and identity
have been creased.
They can deny me justice
but they cannot deny me.

Let it issue.
Let it issue loud and clear.
Let it be heard.
Let it be heard far and near.
Let it sound.
Let it sound so hard it shakes the ground.
Let them stand.
Let them stand tall and proud like a man.
Let it fall.
Let it fall to the ground like a ball.
Let them shiver.
Let them shiver so cold they cry a river.
Let it break.
Let it break until that's all they can take.
And let us build.
Let us build so high we touch the sky.

You'll awake one day and find yourself surrounded by idiots and imbeciles. Those who are with you in the beginning are rarely the ones best suited to guide you in the end. Separate the wheat from the chaff early and be rewarded. Elevate your most reliable to positions of alumni and favored professors so their loyalty may be rewarded too.

There are two types of people. Those who read Machiavelli's *The Prince* as a cautionary tale, and those who see it as a sort of guidebook on proper political behavior. Society should elevate the former and eliminate the latter.

Assassination is often played as a sort of game, so that nobody sees it coming. We saw exactly that in Malaysia and I've seen it first-hand. The executioner laughs you into your grave. He pours you a drink and toasts to your demise, laughing all the while.

Life *is* a sort of game,
but one worth playing seriously.

34

Let no man have a window into your life
that you have not provided.

Like History, many people read
Philosophy incorrectly, attributing Vice to
Virtue and Virtue to Vice.

It is up to us to set the course for the future. Never leave that task to others, lest you be deceived and excluded altogether.

Never forget that your enemies job is to eliminate you, and they'll do a thorough job of it if you let them.

Shake out your curtains every once in a while and see the light anew.

May my enemy be impaled upon his own
ego and her own self-interest.

Drink to clear the cobwebs.
Smoke to revive the spirit.
And let no one scold you for it.

My greatest mistake was in thinking the world would naturally understand me. Misunderstanding is the *casus belli* of the Black Man. Therefore I now define myself explicitly. Do not wonder why.

42

My enemy wishes for my eternal demise.
And still I rise. And still I rise.

They're playing with memory and history.
Identity and personality.
The brain and the body.
Think about that for a second or two.

The hypocrisy, complacency, and complicity of American Media is absolutely appalling.

Defeating the enemy wouldn't be such a
difficult task were it not for
their profound cowardice.

My only caveat to Kaczinsky is that it is not Society that needs liberation from Technology, but Technology that needs liberation from Society. The Social Caste has become the Technological Caste, not the other way around.

The fruits of our labor and the seeds of our discontent do not fall far from one another.

There comes a time in every man's life
when he's got to break from the pack,
separate from the herd,
and go his own way.

Lord grant me self-determination and sovereignty over destiny and design. For those who wish ill of me would have me done in by fate.

50

Let it be said that he was a man of few
words and great wisdom.

Apply minimalism to all things and be repeatedly rewarded.

Yearn not.
Worry not.
Hunger not.
Live only in the wonderful moments.

Life is full of surprises.
Some you'll understand, some you won't.

54

Always keep Bob Marley playing
and the good vibes flowing.

Everyone is dead, until they are alive.

The pleasure of writing is paramount.

A creak in the wood
sends the whole flock aflutter.

There is a medical conspiracy afoot.

Lady & The Tramp
Cinderella
The Lion King

From Senegal to Spain,
Myanmar to Mozambique,
and Hong Kong to Harlem,
voices are being muffled and silenced.

## ABOUT THE AUTHOR

Champion Muthle aka Daniel Maree is an award-winning Writer-Director, Creative and Cultural Strategist, Independent Journalist, Inventor, Philosopher, Creative Technologist, Afro-Futurist, and Social Entrepreneur. He is a Frederick Douglass Scholar and Forbes 30 Under 30 Honoree for Social Entrepreneurship. His work has been featured in the MoMA and the Library of Congress.

www.ingramcontent.com/pod-product-compliance
Lightning Source LLC
Chambersburg PA
CBHW050052260726
48658CB00005B/1907